The Hidden World of

Toilets

Volume

Monika Davies

Consultants

Lisa Ellick, M.A.
Math Specialist
Norfolk Public Schools

Pamela Estrada, M.S. Ed.
Teacher
Westminster School District

Publishing Credits

Rachelle Cracchiolo, M.S.Ed., *Publisher*
Conni Medina, M.A.Ed., *Managing Editor*
Dona Herweck Rice, *Series Developer*
Emily R. Smith, M.A.Ed., *Series Developer*
Diana Kenney, M.A.Ed., NBCT, *Content Director*
Stacy Monsman, M.A., *Editor*
Kristy Stark, M.A.Ed., *Editor*
Kevin Panter, *Graphic Designer*

Image Credits: Front cover, p.1 Claus Alwin Vogel/Getty Images; back cover
Imagemore Co., Ltd./Alamy; p.5 (top left) Vitaliy Markov/Alamy; p.6 Getty Images;
p.8 (bottom) William Robinson/Alamy; p.9 (top) Arcaid Images/Alamy; p.10 (top)
Peter Horree/Alamy; p.10 (bottom) PA Images/Alamy; 11 (both) SSPL/Getty Images;
p.16 (top and middle) © Monica Bonvicini and VG-Bild Kunst. "Don't Miss a Sec',
2004", photo by Jannes Linders; pp.16 (bottom), 17 Zuma Press/Alamy; p.20 Mark
Williamson/Science Photo Library; p.21 (illustration) Timothy J. Bradley; p.23 (right)
Dinodia Photos/Alamy; p.24 courtesy of United Nations; p.25 Europa Newswire/
Alamy; p.26 courtesy of Cranfield Water Science Institute, Cranfield University; p.27
Kumar Sriskandan/Alamy; all other images from iStock and/or Shutterstock.

Library of Congress Cataloging-in-Publication Data

Names: Davies, Monika, author.
Title: The hidden world of toilets / Monika Davies.
Description: Huntington Beach, CA : Teacher Created Materials, [2018] |
    Includes index. | Audience: Grades 4 to 6.
Identifiers: LCCN 2017033188 (print) | LCCN 2017042026 (ebook) | ISBN
    9781425859565 (eBook) | ISBN 9781425858100 (pbk.)
Subjects: LCSH: Toilets--Juvenile literature.
Classification: LCC TH6498 (ebook) | LCC TH6498 .D38 2018 (print) | DDC
    696/.182--dc23
LC record available at https://lccn.loc.gov/2017033188

Teacher Created Materials

5301 Oceanus Drive
Huntington Beach, CA 92649-1030
http://www.tcmpub.com

ISBN 978-1-4258-5810-0

© 2018 Teacher Created Materials, Inc.
Made in China
Nordica.112017.CA21701237

Table of Contents

Toiling Toilets

It is estimated that we spend over $1\frac{1}{2}$ hours on toilets each week. That adds up to almost 92 days over a lifetime! We have a pretty serious relationship with our toilets. But, do we take them for granted?

Our toilets **toil** away for us every day. Yet, they get little thanks for their hard work! At first glance, a toilet is a simple device. It's designed to get rid of human waste. That's it; that's all. However, toilets are critical devices for proper **sanitation**.

Many people view their time on the "porcelain throne" as a regular part of their day. However, this is not the case for everyone. Across the globe, there are still 2.4 billion people who do not have access to toilets. This is a critical global issue. And it is a cause that the United Nations (UN) is supporting. Clean toilets for **developing countries** should be a worldwide priority. But the global community needs to work together to make that happen.

Perhaps you have never thought much about toilets. But, they have a colorful history. When you think of toilets, you probably picture the one in your home. But, toilets can be very different around the world.

Now, let's dive deep into the hidden world of toilets!

These ancient toilet artifacts are on display in a museum in Greece.

This weathered outhouse sits by a path in New England in the United States.

This medieval toilet is located in the castle of Xativa in Spain.

A Whirling History

Throughout history, people have had to deal with human waste. The modern solution is to flush that waste down the toilet. Sewage systems then drag it all far, far away. But, the flushing toilet wasn't always the go-to solution. Over the years, the toilet has taken on many shapes and forms. So, who gets credit for creating the toilet?

Ancient Rome

The toilet's origin story is murky. There is evidence that people from Scotland or Greece may have built the world's first restrooms. But, the ancient Romans built the best aqueducts. Aqueducts are pipe systems that transport water to large cities. They are a great way to import water from faraway sources!

The Romans built many bathhouses and **communal** restrooms. These were large structures that housed long benches where people could sit and "do their business." Rome once had 144 **latrines** and communal restrooms throughout the city!

However, the Romans did not entirely understand good **hygiene**. People could not simply buy toilet paper at a Roman market. Instead, Romans used a communal sponge on a stick to clean themselves. Unfortunately, this practice spread bacteria from person to person.

This illustration shows a nineteenth-century Roman with servants in a communal bathroom.

Scientists estimate that Roman aqueducts carried about 60 cubic meters of water per minute. Imagine that a rectangular prism is filled with 60 cubic meters of water. It has a height of 5 meters. What are all the possible dimensions of its base? Draw and label models to prove your solutions.

public latrines in ancient Rome

England

Before flush toilets and restrooms, people turned to chamber pots to do their business. These containers were used as **portable** toilets. People often kept them under their beds.

In medieval England, most people used these age-old chamber pots. But, the evolution of the toilet made its next leap in a bigger way. During this time, the garderobe (GAR-drohb) officially entered the toilet world. It was a unique—and smelly—addition to castle homes.

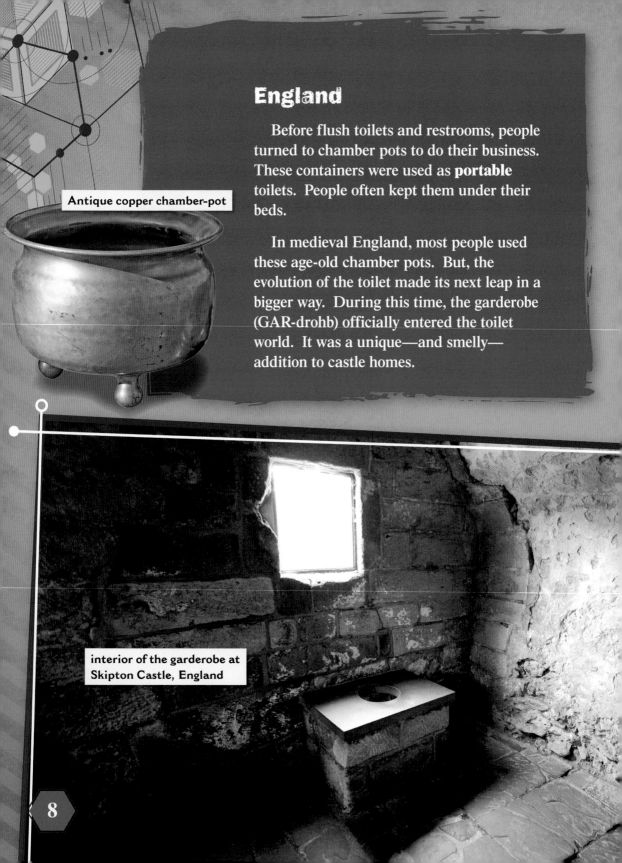

Antique copper chamber-pot

interior of the garderobe at Skipton Castle, England

Garderobes are small rooms tucked into the sides of castles. They can be seen sticking out from the castles. People would go into the room to do their business. Then, the garderobe used gravity to funnel waste away! Some later castles even had garderobes that emptied into the castle's moat.

So, what makes the garderobe so special? Think about the buildings in your city. Most of them have toilets. And, the architects who designed the buildings likely thought about where to put the toilet first. But, medieval England marked the first time and place architects thought about where the toilet should go.

The garderobe at Beauman's Castle in Great Britain sticks out of the wall.

LET'S EXPLORE MATH

Imagine that a builder in medieval England is doubling the height of the stone wall behind a garderobe, but keeping the other dimensions the same. Each stone is 1 cubic meter. Use the picture of the original wall to answer the questions.

original wall

1. What are the dimensions of the taller wall? Draw and label a model to prove your solution.

2. How does the volume of the new wall compare to the volume of the original wall?

The Birth of the Flush Toilet

In 1596, the world's first flush toilet was made by Sir John Harington. He was the godson of Queen Elizabeth I. He had an idea for a new toilet. His idea used a bowl filled with water from an upstairs **cistern**, or tank. Human waste was flushed away when the bowl's pipe **valve** was released. The Queen had this modern "water closet" installed in her Richmond home.

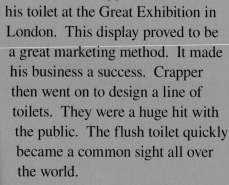

Sir John Harington

However, the flush toilet was years away from being a popular household device. Harington's invention needed 7.5 gallons (28 liters) of water to flush away waste. That's a lot of water! Most people in the 16th century would not have wanted to waste this much water. (Today's toilets use less than 2 gal. (8 L) of water per flush.)

The first flush toilet offered to the public was made by Thomas Crapper. (Yes, that is his real name!) In 1851, Crapper showcased his toilet at the Great Exhibition in London. This display proved to be a great marketing method. It made his business a success. Crapper then went on to design a line of toilets. They were a huge hit with the public. The flush toilet quickly became a common sight all over the world.

Thomas Crapper

painted toilet from 1880

This advertisement for Thomas Crapper's new toilet is from his 1902 catalog.

LET'S EXPLORE MATH

Thomas Crapper's toilet tank had dimensions (in inches) of about $20 \times 10 \times 11$. John Harington's tank had about twice the volume. What is a possible set of dimensions that Harington could have used if his tank was shaped like a rectangular prism? Use words, numbers, or pictures to prove your solution.

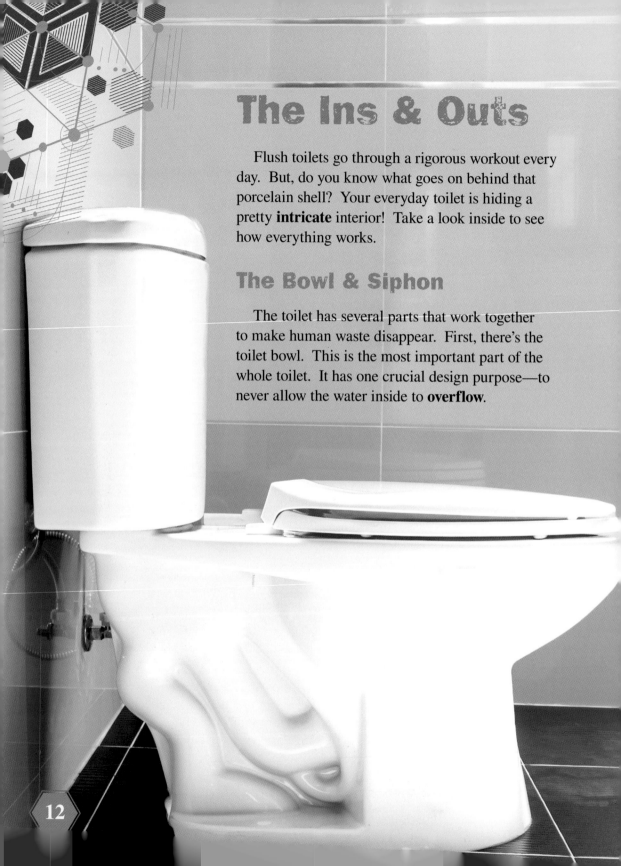

The Ins & Outs

Flush toilets go through a rigorous workout every day. But, do you know what goes on behind that porcelain shell? Your everyday toilet is hiding a pretty **intricate** interior! Take a look inside to see how everything works.

The Bowl & Siphon

The toilet has several parts that work together to make human waste disappear. First, there's the toilet bowl. This is the most important part of the whole toilet. It has one crucial design purpose—to never allow the water inside to **overflow**.

12

Notice the S-shaped pipe that leaves the toilet bowl. This is the toilet's siphon. When you flush a toilet, water flows into the bowl to wash away waste, odor, and germs. The siphon's job is to make sure that the bowl always has the same level of water. As water runs into the bowl, the siphon tube fills. The siphon then acts quickly, sucking the extra water out of the toilet bowl. This creates that flush noise that people know and love! Even if you pour several gallons of water in a toilet bowl, it will never overflow. This is helpful in preventing restroom floods!

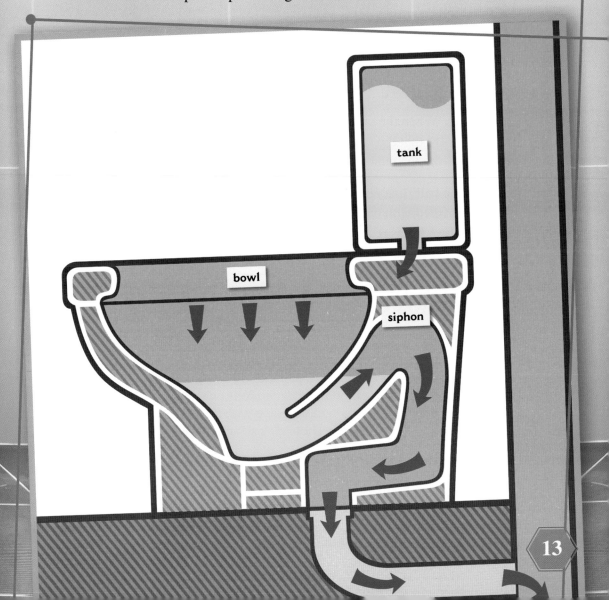

The Flush & Refill

A tank sits above each toilet bowl. Inside the tank are tubes and valves submerged in water. The tank of water is what jump-starts the flush in the toilet bowl.

When you push a toilet's handle, you're actually pulling a chain that opens the flush valve. The flush valve in the tank of water opens and floods the toilet bowl. Over a gallon (4 liters) of water is released into the bowl, filling the siphon tube, to flush away human waste. This all happens in a few seconds!

You've probably noticed you can't flush a toilet immediately after the first flush. This is because the tank of water needs to refill. The toilet tank has a **mechanism** called a ball float. This piece hovers on top of the water in the tank. When the tank of water empties, the ball drops. This signals the refill valve that the tank is low on water. The refill valve then begins slowly refilling the tank with water, which also raises the ball float.

Once the ball float returns to its original location, the refill valve knows the tank is filled with enough water to complete its next flush. And, just like that, the toilet is ready for use once again!

LET'S EXPLORE MATH

Suppose your parents are having a plumber replace the toilet tank in your home. The plumber gives them the dimensions (in inches) of three possible tanks. Your parents want to install the one with the least volume. Which of the following tanks should they choose? Explain your reasoning.

    A. $17 \times 8 \times 15$

    B. $18 \times 8 \times 14$

    C. $20 \times 8 \times 13$

Flushing Mechanism

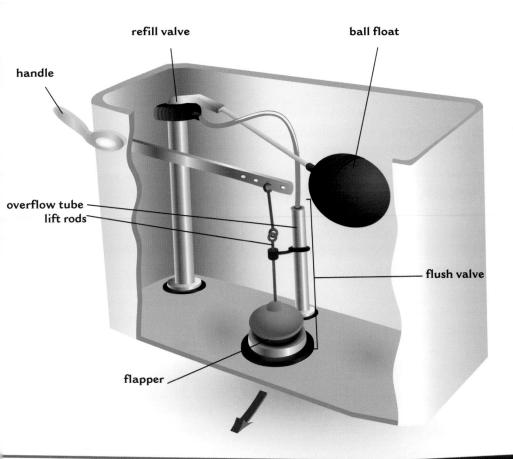

refill valve

ball float

handle

overflow tube

lift rods

flush valve

flapper

Global Toilets

Toilets around the world come in all shapes, colors, and sizes. Many countries have modern toilets that range from simple to wacky. Let's take a worldwide road trip as we take a look at toilets from around the globe!

Unique London Loo

Don't Miss a Sec was installed in 2004. This London restroom sat right in the bustle of a crowded street. Monica Bonvinci designed this unique loo. (*Loo* is the British word for "restroom" or "toilet".) One-way mirrors surround the toilet. This means no one can see in, but users can see out! This gives users the chance to watch **passersby** while on the toilet. Bonvinci's idea was that, even if you had to go to the restroom, you could still watch the action outside the structure. Still, it takes a brave soul to use this toilet!

Porcelain Palace in China

China lays claim to the world's largest restroom, and you can find it in the city of Chongqing (chuhng-CHEENG). It is housed in a building that is four stories tall and has over one thousand toilets! The building has been called the Porcelain Palace.

inside *Don't Miss a Sec*

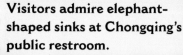
outside *Don't Miss a Sec*

Visitors admire elephant-shaped sinks at Chongqing's public restroom.

Monica Bonvinci's *Don't Miss a Sec* is a rectangular prism. It has a length of about 7 feet, a width of about 6 feet, and a height of about 8 feet.

What are four other possible sets of dimensions the artist could use if she wants to build new structures with the same volume?

Porcelain Palace

Two Choices in Japan

If you travel to Japan, you will likely stumble upon two types of toilets: Japanese style and Western style.

Japanese-style toilets are also known as squat toilets. Common in Asian countries, squat toilets function the same as toilets in Western countries. However, you squat instead of sit. Squat toilets are the most common type of toilet found in public restrooms in Japan. That's because they are often cheaper to make and easier to clean.

In Japan, squat toilets are built into the floor.

The Western-style toilet is Japan's take on the modern toilet. But, the Japanese version comes with a few more bells and whistles. There is a button panel beside the toilet. Users have many choices to make sure their bottoms are extra clean! They can choose from several water spray options. They can also choose how much water is needed to wash waste away. Water temperature controls are offered for maximum comfort. There is also a fan that dries away water **residue**. Bottoms are left feeling squeaky clean. And, people don't need as much toilet paper. That's not all. Some electronic toilets even have heated seats and play music!

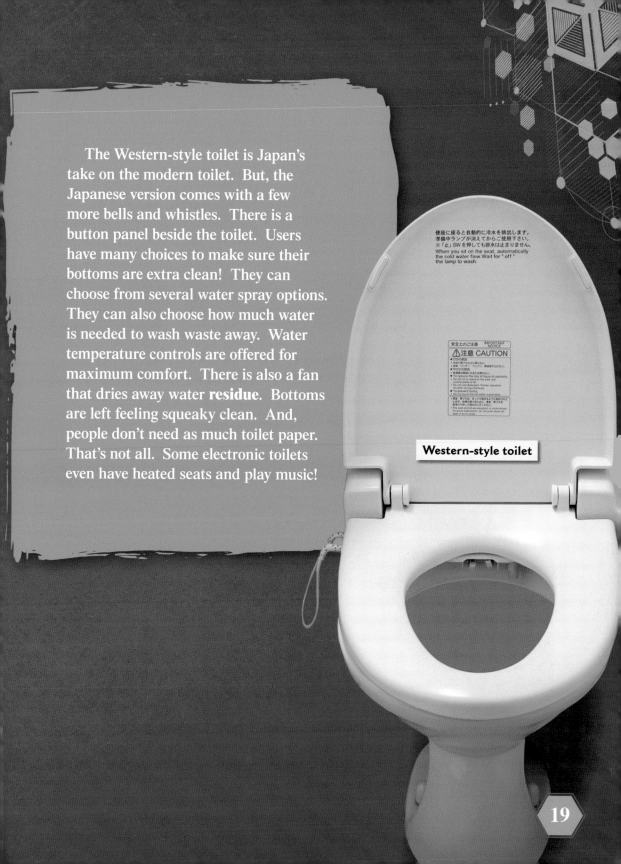

便座に座ると自動的に冷水を排出します。
準備中ランプが消えてからご使用下さい。
※「止」SWを押しても排水は止まりません。
When you sit on the seat, automatically
the cold water flow. Wait for " off "
the lamp to wash.

安全上のご注意 IMPORTANT NOTICE
⚠注意 CAUTION

Western-style toilet

Out-of-This-World Toilets

Astronauts have an out-of-this-world time when they head into space. But, they still need restroom breaks when they're orbiting the globe. So, how exactly does a toilet work in space?

Toilets on Earth rely on gravity and the fact that all things are pulled downward. But in space, things are different. Everything floats up and away—including waste! Luckily, the solution is simple. Space toilets use vacuums to suck away waste.

When astronauts need to **urinate**, they use a funnel attached to a tube. This funnel is made for both men and women. The tube is attached to the toilet. A vacuum sucks the liquid down the tube into the toilet. Astronauts don't need to sit to use the tube. They can stand or even hang upside down!

space shuttle toilet

Sometimes, astronauts need to sit down to do their business. Each sit-down toilet comes equipped with foot straps and a thigh bar to prevent users from floating away. Astronauts just need to make sure there is a strong seal between their bodies and the toilet. Otherwise, the toilet's vacuum will not work. Does that sound complicated? That's why astronauts attend toilet training before leaving for space.

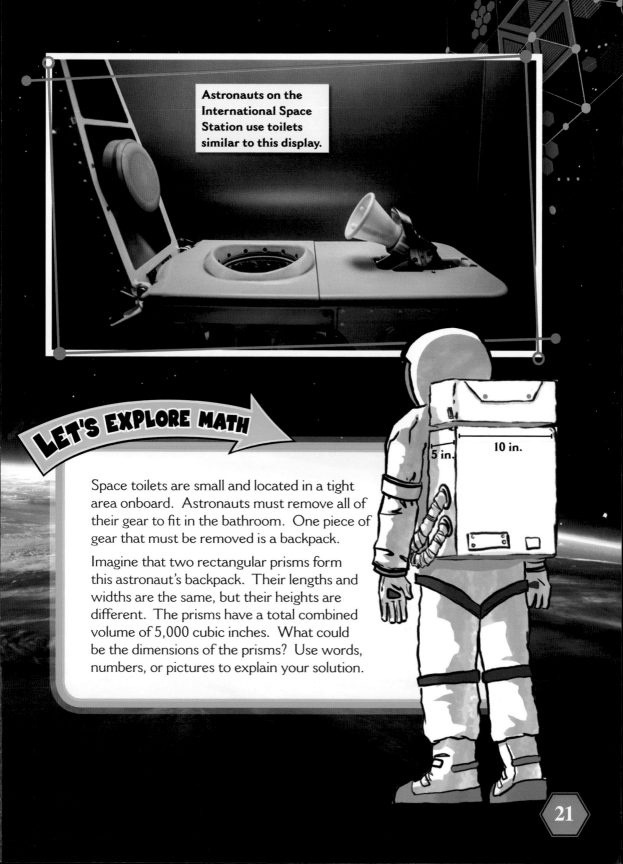

Astronauts on the International Space Station use toilets similar to this display.

10 in.

5 in.

LET'S EXPLORE MATH

Space toilets are small and located in a tight area onboard. Astronauts must remove all of their gear to fit in the bathroom. One piece of gear that must be removed is a backpack.

Imagine that two rectangular prisms form this astronaut's backpack. Their lengths and widths are the same, but their heights are different. The prisms have a total combined volume of 5,000 cubic inches. What could be the dimensions of the prisms? Use words, numbers, or pictures to explain your solution.

Herdsman in the Trans-Alai mountain range in Asia set up this toilet with sheets and wooden boards.

People in the Australian outback used tall metal sheets and a plastic barrel to build this toilet.

Toilets in Developing Nations

Users can choose from a large variety of toilets. One thing they have in common, though, is price. Toilets all cost money. Many of them are artistic, modern wonders. But these toilets do not come cheap. The cost of a Japanese-style electronic toilet seat starts at around $150. A NASA space toilet can cost up to $30 million. Even a normal toilet will cost at least $130.

And, what about people in countries that can't afford these hefty price tags? Modern toilets need clean water to work and good plumbing systems to flush out waste.

People in Zambia tied branches to brush to make this public toilet.

People in Mumbai, India made this toilet out of recycled scraps.

For residents in developed countries, trips to the toilet are part of daily routines. Yet, this is not the case for more than 2.4 billion people around the globe. One out of every three people in the world do not have safe and clean toilets to use.

Nigeria

In Nigeria, about 7 out of 10 people do not have access to clean toilets. That is over 130 million people! Instead, many people **defecate** in the open. They use public fields, lakes, or side streets. They have no other choice. Even if there is a toilet for them to use, it is often dirty or poorly made. This condition spreads germs and diseases.

Clean toilets are central to a person's health. Waste is full of bacteria. Toilets quickly take bacteria away from places where people live, breathe, drink, and eat. Without toilets, bacteria spreads. Bacteria can enter food and drinking water, and they can become **contaminated**. They can make people sick. People may even die.

The UN sees the value of clean and safe toilet access. That is why it has made clean toilets its sixth **Sustainable** Development Goal. Its plan is for everyone around the world to have access to toilets by 2030.

To make this goal a reality, the UN established World Toilet Day in 2013. World Toilet Day builds awareness. It is observed each year on November 19. The day is spent encouraging people to take action. Support is shown for those around the world in need of help.

So, what can you do to help? Talk about the value of clean toilets. Toilets are often a **taboo** topic. People don't like to talk about them. However, people can't help solve problems when they don't know the problems exist.

Members of the United Nations meet to discuss World Toilet Day.

A group of people in New York are some of the first to observe World Toilet Day in 2014.

TOILETS SAVE LIVES!

WORLD TOILET DAY
19 NOVEMBER
BE THANKFUL YOU HAVE A SAFE AND CLEAN TOILET.
2.5 BILLION PEOPLE IN THE WORLD ARE NOT SO LUCKY.

JOIN THE CONVERSATION

Toilets for Tomorrow

Engineers are working to solve other problems with waste. Toilets still use about 2 gal. (8 L) of water per flush. Engineers are working to reduce this amount. In 2012, a team began working on a new type of toilet. A composting toilet sucks water out of waste. The toilet then turns that waste into **fertilizer**. This fertilizer can be added to the soil of trees and gardens to help them grow. Best of all, the toilet uses about 0.2 gal. (1 L) of water per flush to work. This saves a lot of water.

This level of change will take time. Change can happen when everyone pitches in. New toilet technology can help, too. Awareness and innovation will, hopefully, change the world—one toilet at a time.

This Nano Membrane Toilet is being developed to clean waste at home.

THIS IS A
·COMPOSTING TOILET·

IT RECYCLES HUMAN WASTE . . .

Solids and liquids are biologically converted into fertilizer.

IT REPLICATES NATURAL BIOLOGICAL PROCESSES . . .

Oxygen is drawn through moistened wood shavings to create an environment in which bacteria break down organic matter without unpleasant odor.

THIS ENVIRONMENTALLY FRIENDLY TOILET DOES NOT USE WATER . . .

This composter saves the water required for flushing a standard toilet.

THIS IS A WATERLESS TOILET, PLEASE . . .

- DO NOT PUT matches, cigarettes or cigars in this toilet.
- Dispose of trash and inorganic items in appropriate containers.
- Use only toilet paper.
- Close the toilet lid after use.

COMPOSTING TOILETS SAVE WATER IN HOMES, CABINS, BUSINESSES AND PUBLIC FACILITIES!

Restroom Solutions, Inc.
1-800-678-0284

PLEASE CLOSE LID
AFTER USE

This is a composting toilet in Arizona.

🔩 Problem Solving

What happens when nature calls while you are actually out in nature? One option is a portable toilet. These devices are often called camping toilets because of their popularity in tents and cabins. But, they are used in other places, such as boats and recreational vehicles. Hikers even take these toilets with them on long treks.

Imagine that you work for an outdoor equipment company. The camping toilets your company sells have storage tanks shaped like rectangular prisms. You have been tasked with designing and writing the page in the new catalog featuring these products and answering customer questions.

1. Find the missing product specifications describing each toilet.

2. Put the toilets in order from least to greatest volume.

3. Customers call and email with questions. How would you respond to each one?

   a. Do any of the toilets' bases have the same area? Do they also have the same volume? Why or why not?

   b. Which toilet do you recommend for hikers, who will move the toilet frequently? Why?

   c. Which toilet do you recommend for cabin owners who will not move the toilet once it is in place? Why?

Camping Toilet Specifications

Toilet	Length (inches)	Width (inches)	Height (inches)	Area of Base (square inches)	Volume (cubic inches)
A	12	16	14		
B	13	12			2,652
C		15	12	195	
D		15	15		2,925
E	17		14		3,808

Glossary

cistern—a container that holds a supply of water

communal—shared by a community

contaminated—dangerous, dirty, or impure

defecate—to empty solid waste out of the body

developing countries—nations with low economic levels

fertilizer— a substance used in soil to make plants grow better

hygiene— the things used to keep the body clean and healthy

intricate—having many small parts and details

latrines—outdoor toilets

mechanism—a mechanical part with a particular function

overflow—to come over the edge of a container

passersby—people who walk past something or someone

portable—easily moved

residue—a small amount of something left over

sanitation—the process of keeping an area clean

sustainable—able to last or continue for a long time

taboo—not allowed or acceptable

toil—work hard for a long time

urinate—to empty liquid waste out of the body

valve—a mechanical part that controls the flow of air or liquid